EASY PIANO

JERSEY BOYS

The story of Frankie Valli & The Four Seasons

ISBN 978-1-4768-6875-2

HAL•LEONARD®
CORPORATION

7777 W. BLUEMOUND RD. P.O. BOX 13819 MILWAUKEE, WI 53213

Visit Hal Leonard Online at
www.halleonard.com

BIG GIRLS DON'T CRY

Words and Music by BOB CREWE
and BOB GAUDIO

Moderately

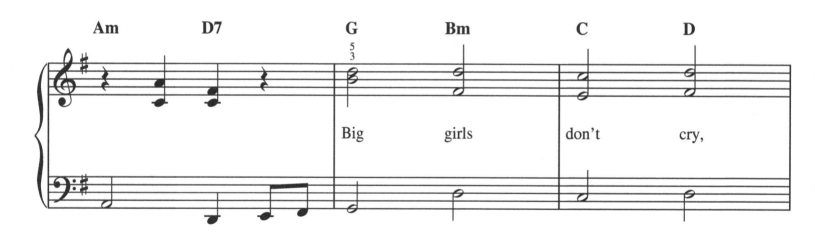

Big   girls   don't   cry,

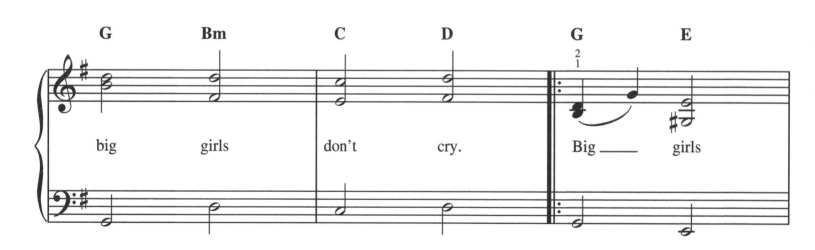

big   girls   don't   cry.   Big ____ girls

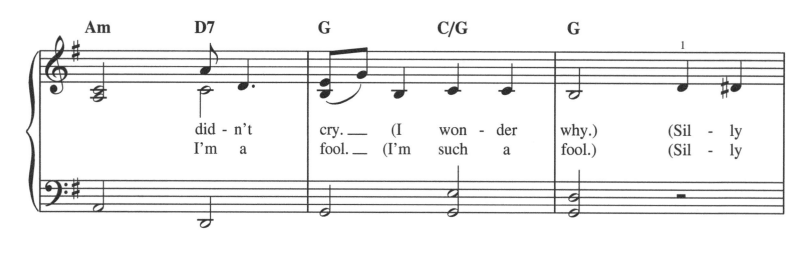

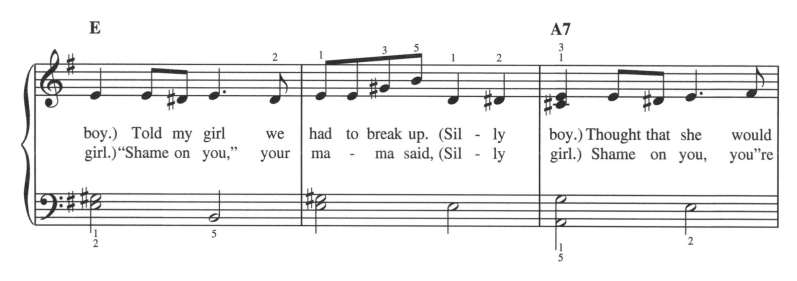

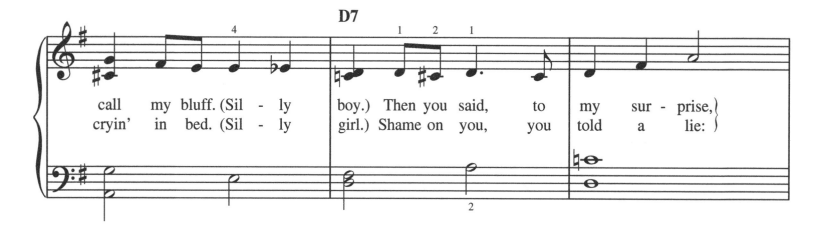

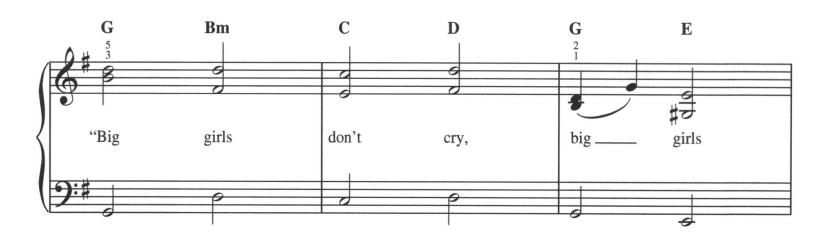

BIG MAN IN TOWN

Words and Music by
BOB GAUDIO

Medium Rock

(Big man in town) Each day as
town) They think that

I grow old - er, the nights are get - ting cold - er.
I'm a rov - er, but my ro - vin' days are o - ver.

Some - day the sun will shine on me.
Some day your folks will wel - come me.

BYE BYE BABY
(Baby Goodbye)

Words and Music by BOB CREWE
and BOB GAUDIO

Bye, bye, ba - by, ba - by, good - bye. _____

Bye, bye, ba - by, don't make me

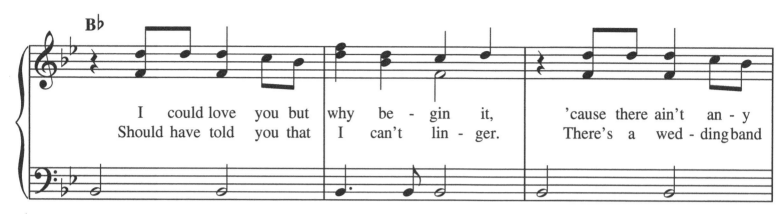

I could love you but why be - gin it, 'cause there ain't an - y
Should have told you that I can't lin - ger. There's a wed - ding band

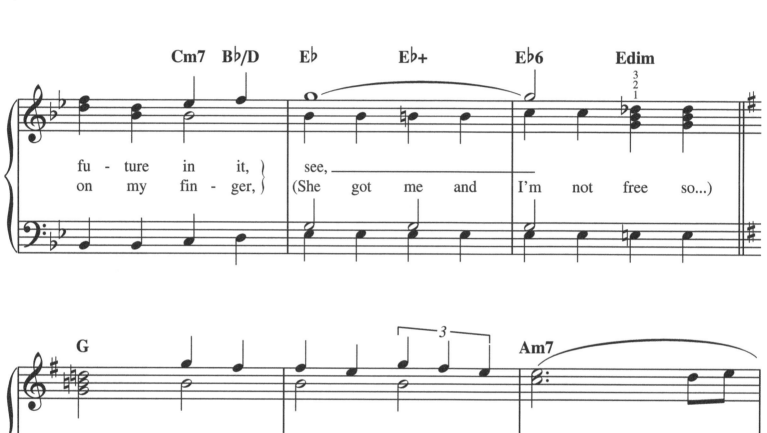

fu - ture in it, see, (She got me and I'm not free so...)
on my fin - ger,

Bye, bye, ba - by, ba - by, good - bye.

Bye, bye, ba - by, don't make me

CAN'T TAKE MY EYES OFF OF YOU

Words and Music by BOB CREWE
and BOB GAUDIO

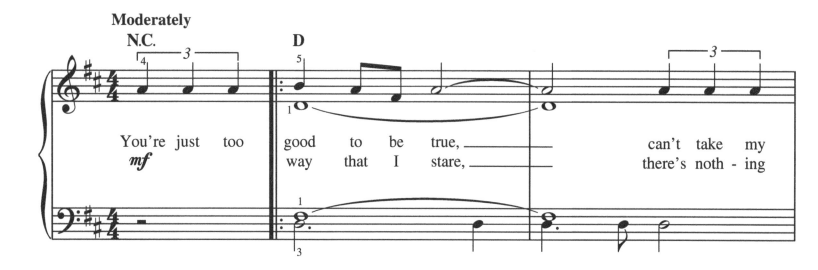

Moderately

You're just too good to be true, can't take my
way that I stare, there's noth - ing

eyes off of you. You'd be like heav - en to touch,
else to com - pare. The sight of you leaves me weak,

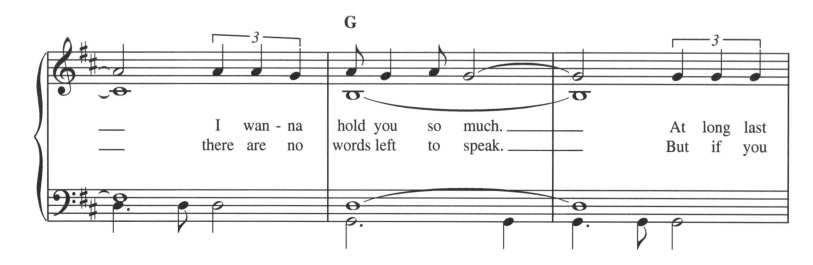

I wan - na hold you so much. At long last
there are no words left to speak. But if you

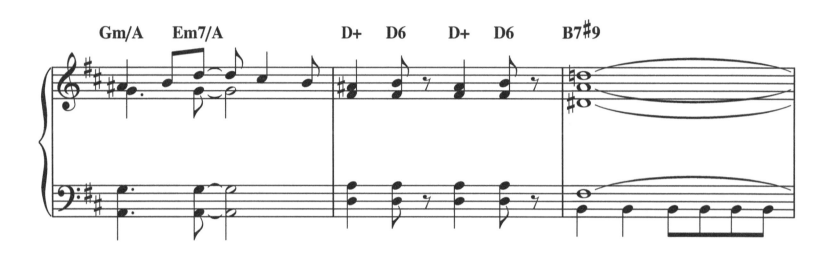

I love you ba - by, __ and if it's quite all right, __ I need you,

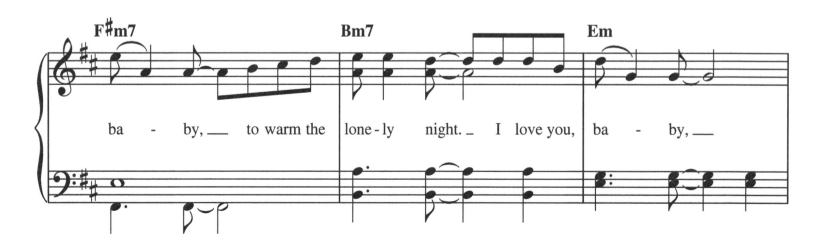

ba - by, __ to warm the lone - ly night. __ I love you, ba - by, __

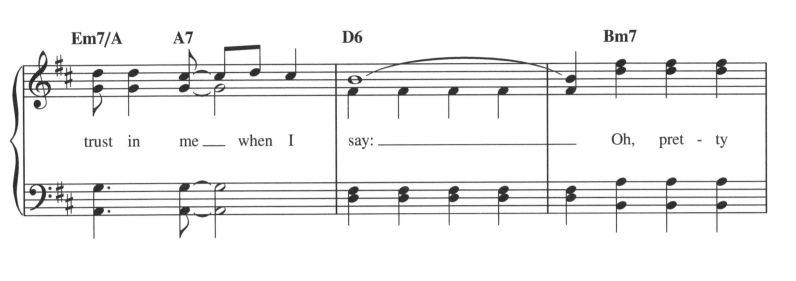

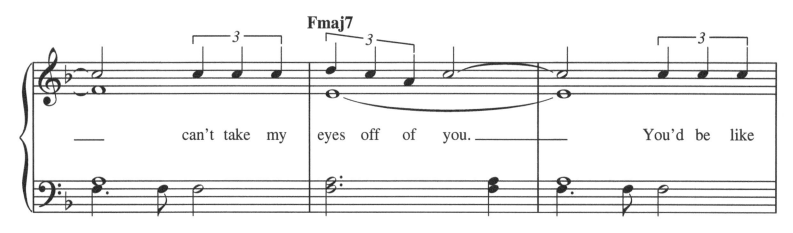

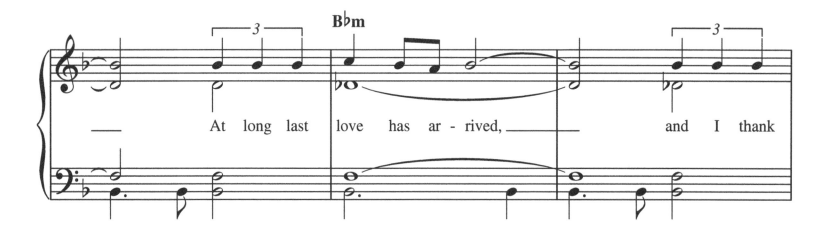

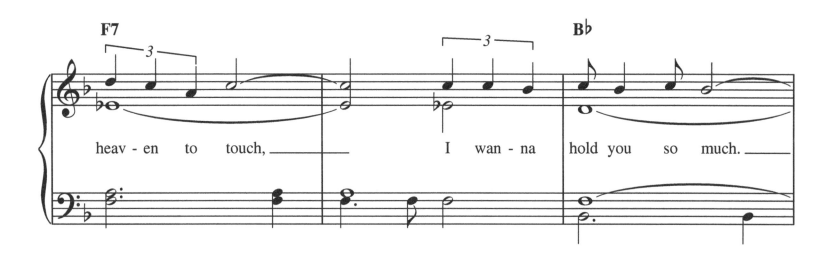

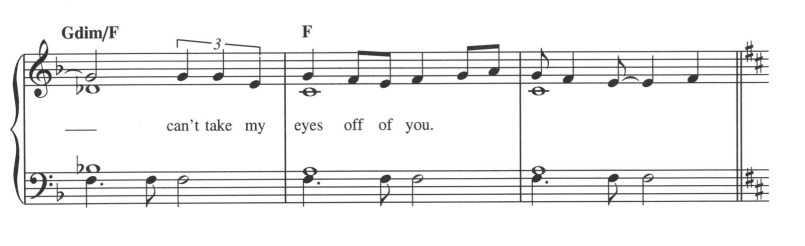

can't take my eyes off of you.

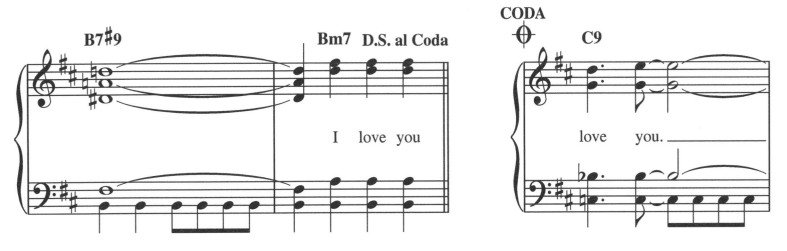

I love you

CODA

love you. _____

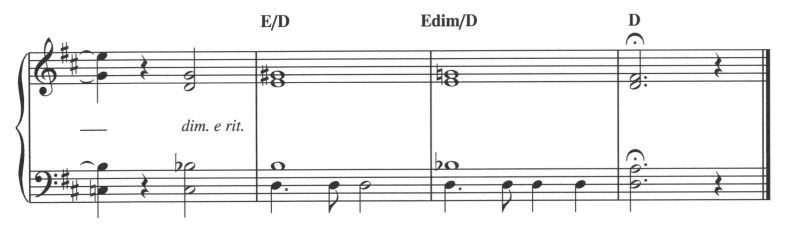

dim. e rit.

DECEMBER 1963
(Oh, What a Night)

Words and Music by ROBERT GAUDIO
and JUDY PARKER

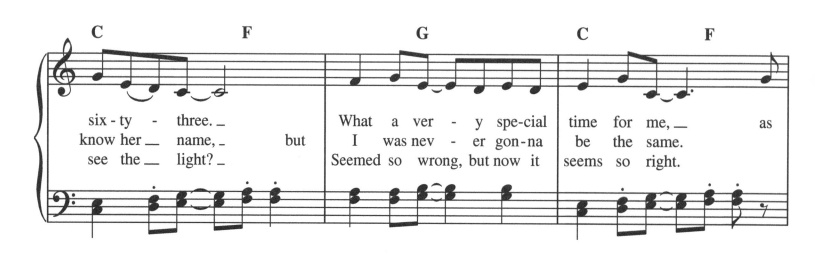

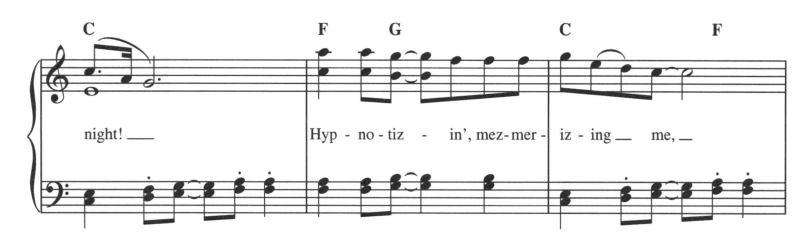

night! ___   Hyp - no - tiz - in', mez - mer - iz - ing ___ me, ___

she was ev - 'ry-thing I dreamed she'd be. ___ Sweet sur-ren - der, what a

night.

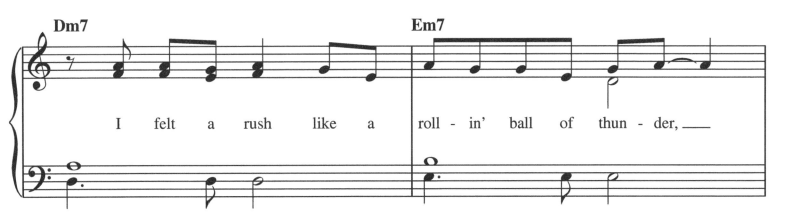

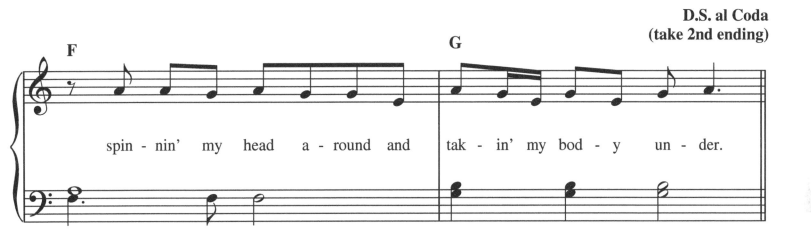

S. al Coda
(take 2nd ending)

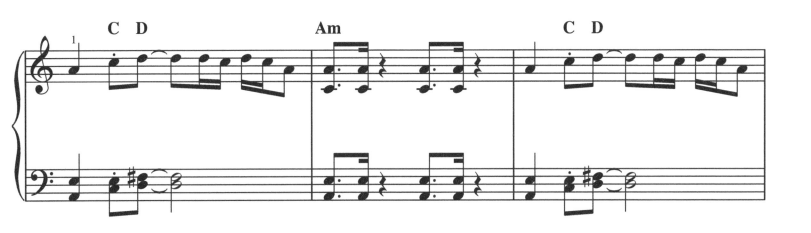

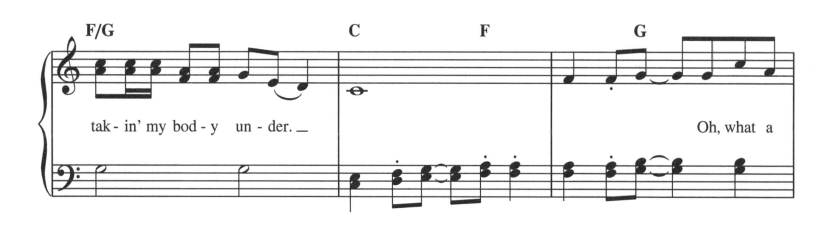

FALLEN ANGEL

Words and Music by GUY FLETCHER
and DOUG FLETT

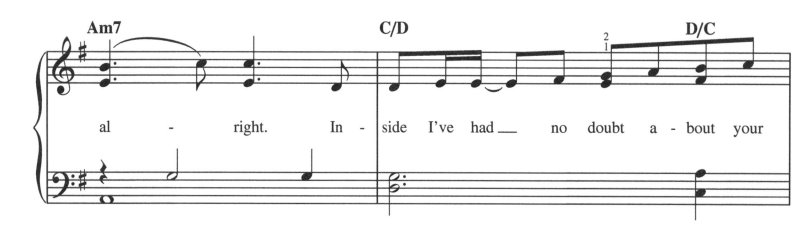

al - right. In - side I've had ___ no doubt a - bout your

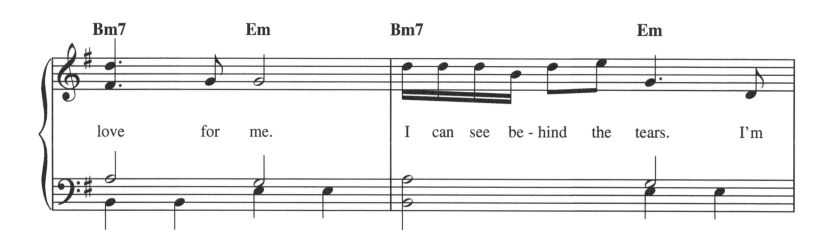

love for me. I can see be - hind the tears. I'm

cer - tain of the way we feel and, giv - en time, the hurt will heal. I

need ___ you. I think I al - ways will. From

home a - gain, so won't you close ___ the door. Stay

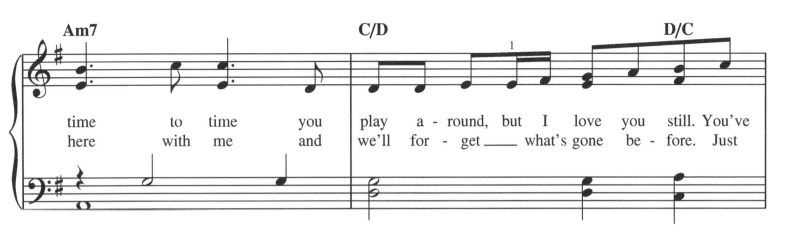

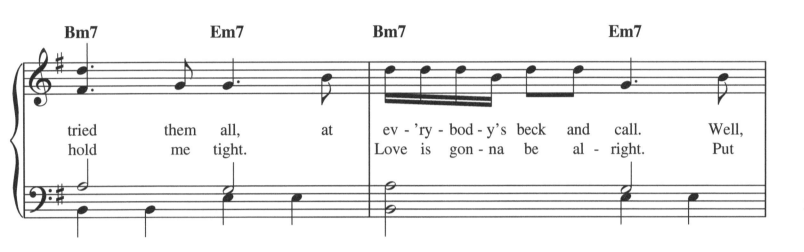

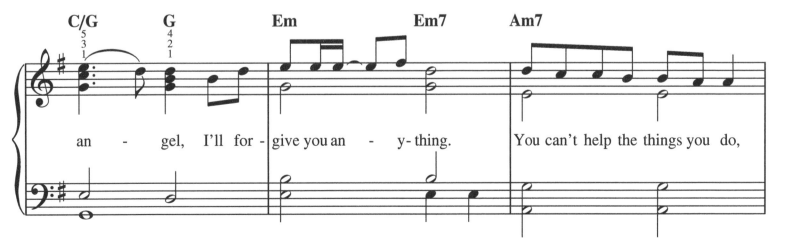

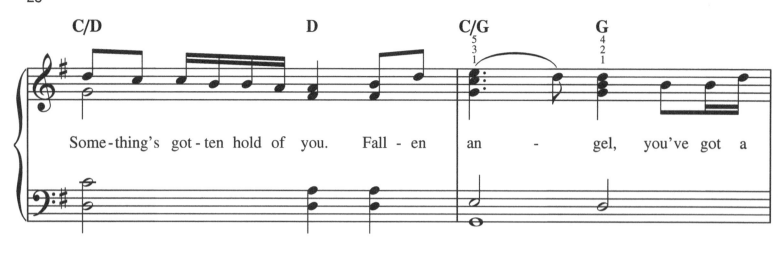

Some-thing's got-ten hold of you. Fall-en an - gel, you've got a

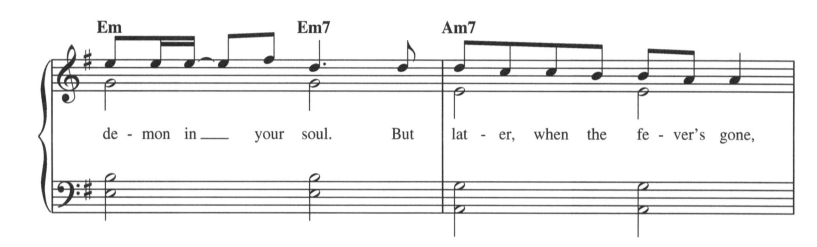

de - mon in ___ your soul. But lat - er, when the fe - ver's gone,

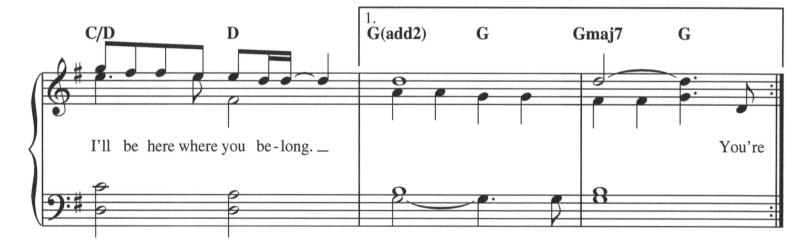

I'll be here where you be-long. ____ You're

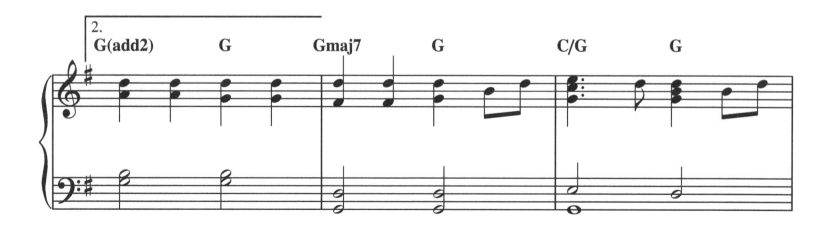

LET'S HANG ON

Words and Music by BOB CREWE,
DENNY RANDELL and SANDY LINZER

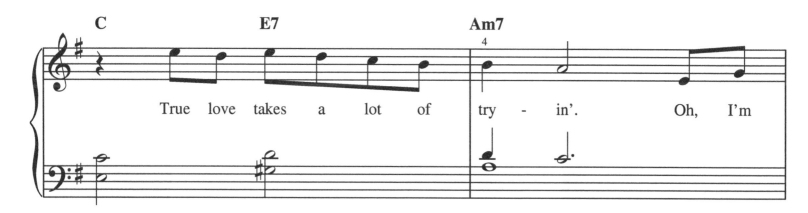

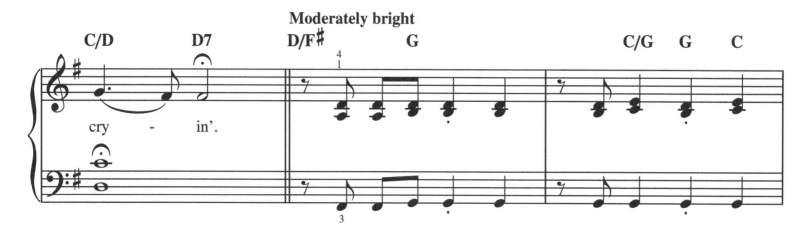

to what we've got. ___ Don't let go, ___ girl; we've got a

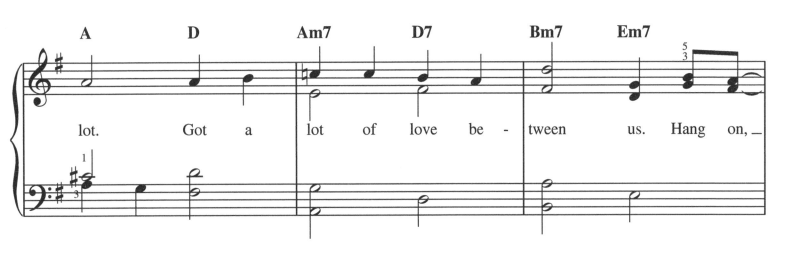

lot. Got a lot of love be - tween us. Hang on, ___

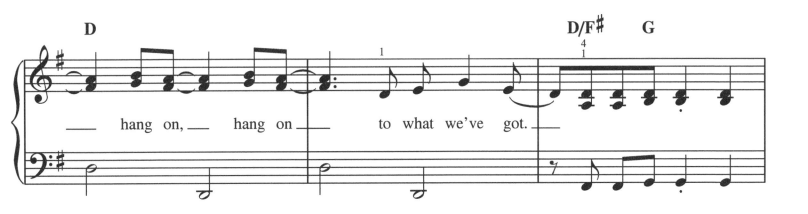

___ hang on, ___ hang on ___ to what we've got. ___

You say you're gon - na go and call it quits, __ gon - na
There is - n't an - y - thing I would - n't do. __ I'd pay

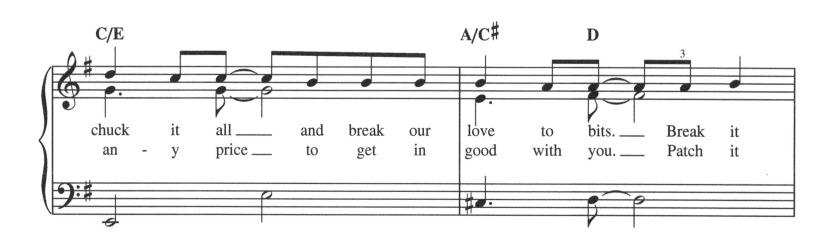

chuck it all ___ and break our love to bits. __ Break it
an - y price ___ to get in good with you. __ Patch it

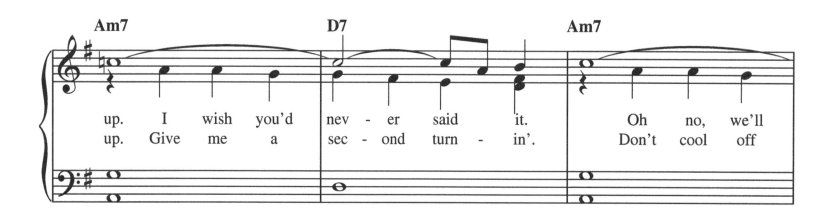

up. I wish you'd nev - er said it. Oh no, we'll
up. Give me a sec - ond turn - in'. Don't cool off

both re - gret it. That lit - tle chip of dia - mond
while I'm burn - in'. You've got me cry - in', dy - in'

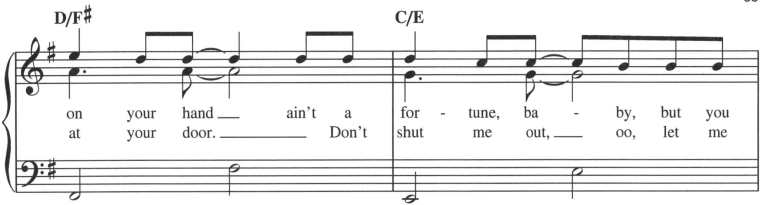

on your hand ___ ain't a for - tune, ba - by, but you
at your door. _____ Don't shut me out, ___ oo, let me

know it stands ___ for the love, a love to
in once more. ___ O - pen up, your arms I

tie and bind ya; we just can't leave be - hind us. }
need to hold you, your heart, oh, girl, I love you }

Ba - by, ___ don't you know? _____ Don't you go, think it o - ver and

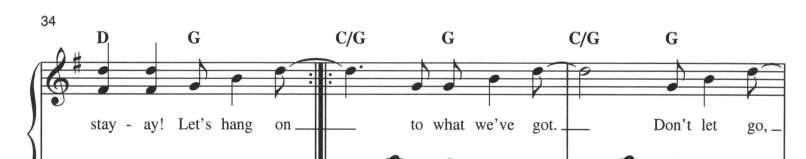

stay - ay! Let's hang on ___ ___ to what we've got. ___ Don't let go, ___

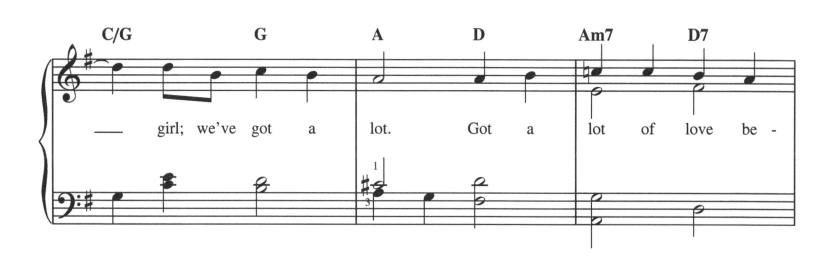

___ girl; we've got a lot. Got a lot of love be -

tween us. Hang on, ___ hang on, ___ hang on... ___ Let's hang on ___

1.

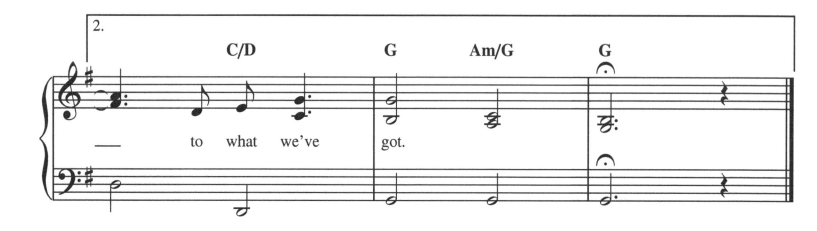

2.

___ to what we've got.

STAY

Words and Music by
MAURICE WILLIAMS

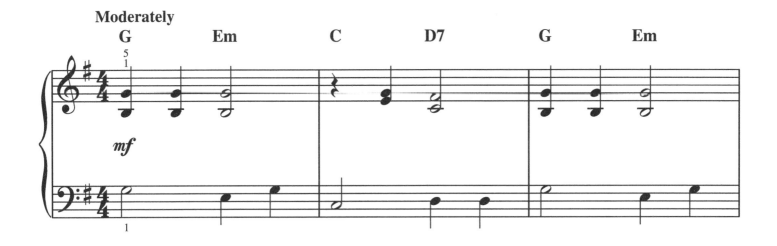

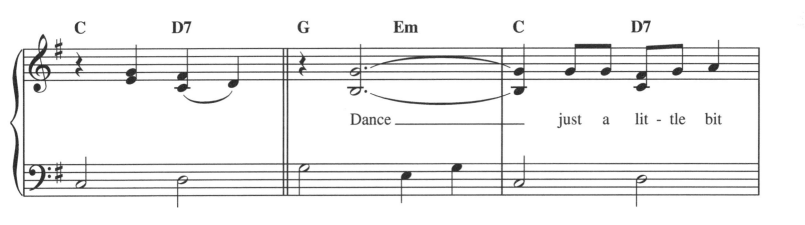

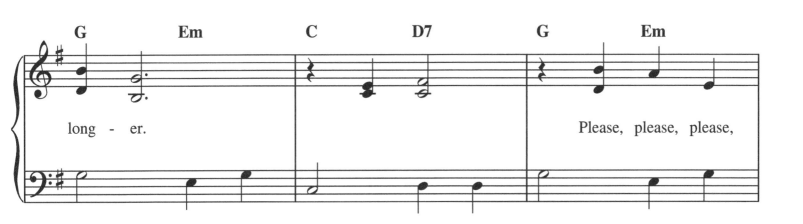

please   tell me that you're   go - in' to.   Now your

dad - dy don't   mind,   and your   mom-my don't   mind.

(L.H. 8va lower to end)

Could   we   have an - oth - er   dance,   dear,

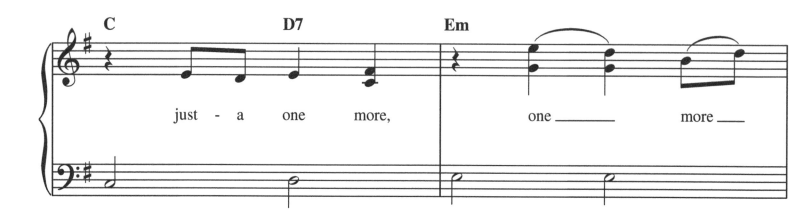

just - a   one   more,   one _____   more _____

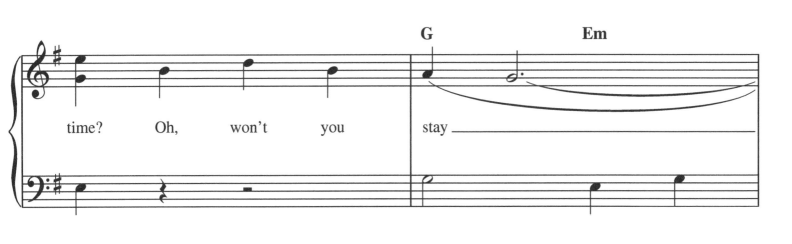

time? Oh, won't you stay _____

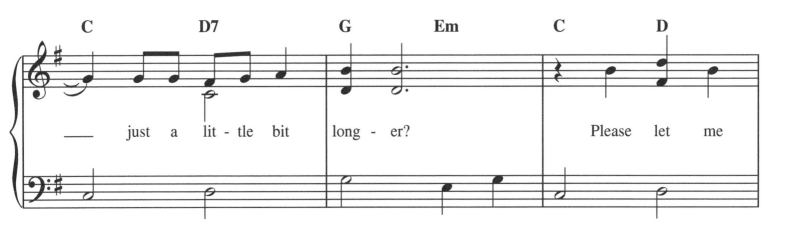

_____ just a lit - tle bit long - er? Please let me

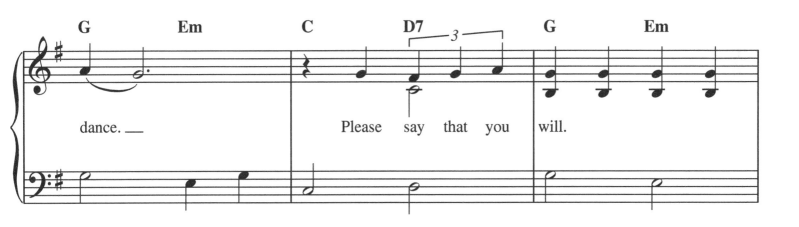

dance. ___ Please say that you will.

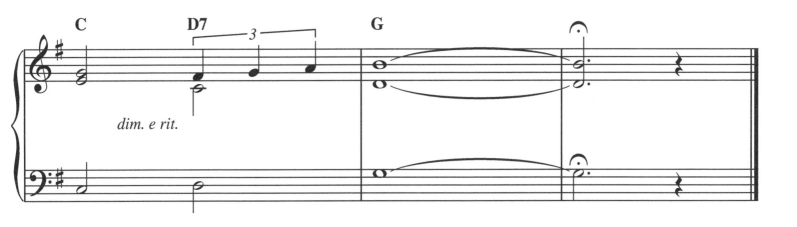

dim. e rit.

MY BOYFRIEND'S BACK

Words and Music by ROBERT FELDMAN,
GERALD GOLDSTEIN and RICHARD GOTTEHRER

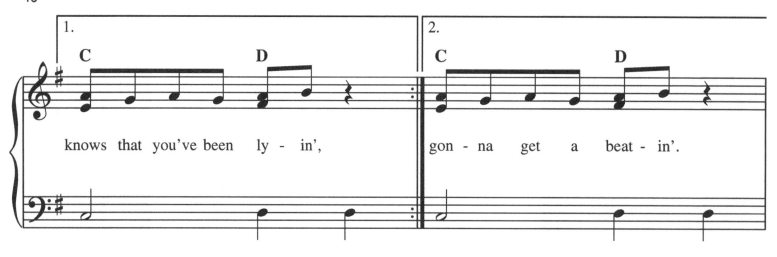

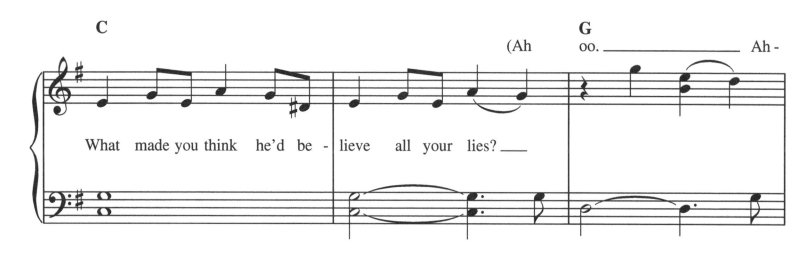

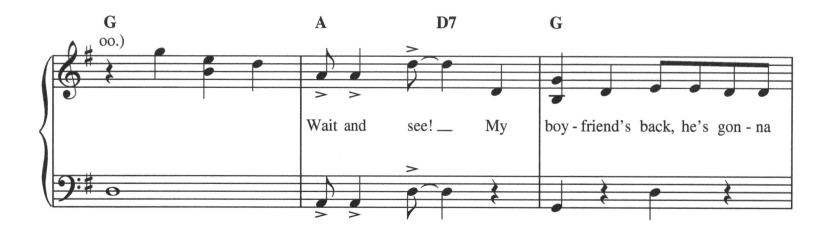

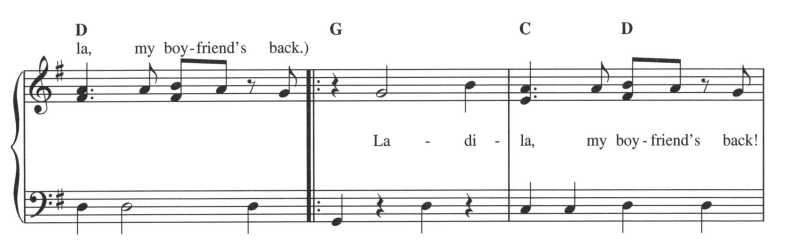

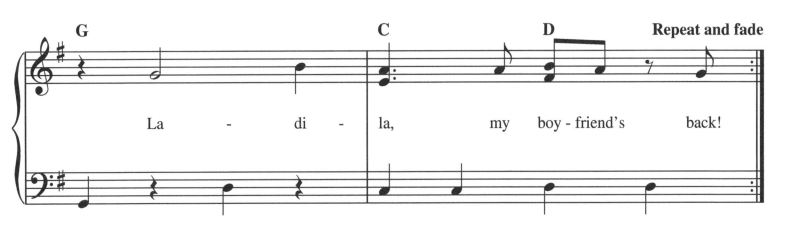

MY EYES ADORED YOU

Words and Music by BOB CREWE
and KENNY NOLAN

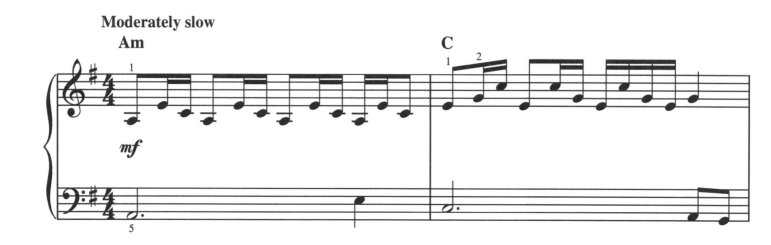

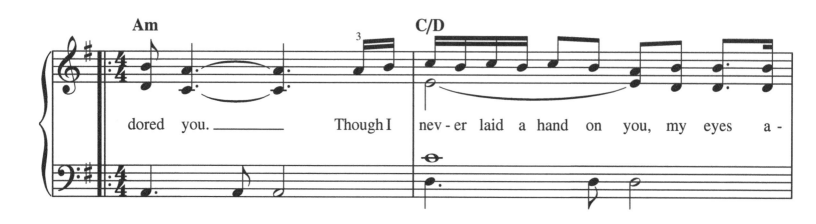

when we came to be.
made my-self a name.

Walk-ing home ev-'ry day o - ver
Fun-ny I seem to find that no

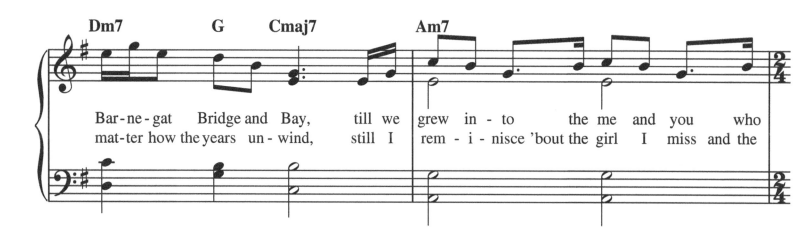

Bar-ne-gat Bridge and Bay, till we
mat-ter how the years un-wind, still I

grew in-to the me and you who
rem-i-nisce 'bout the girl I miss and the

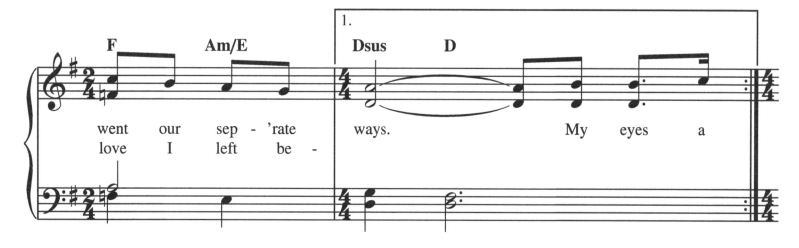

1.

went our sep - 'rate ways.
love I left be -

My eyes a

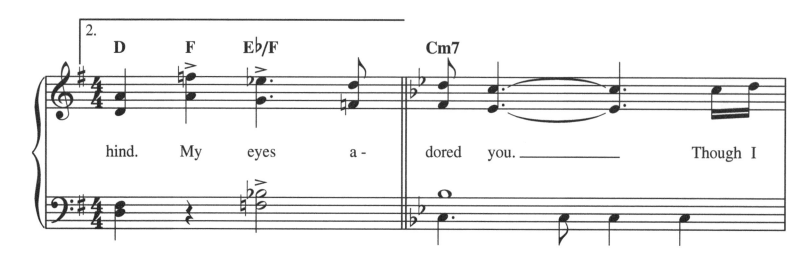

2.

hind. My eyes a - dored you. _____ Though I

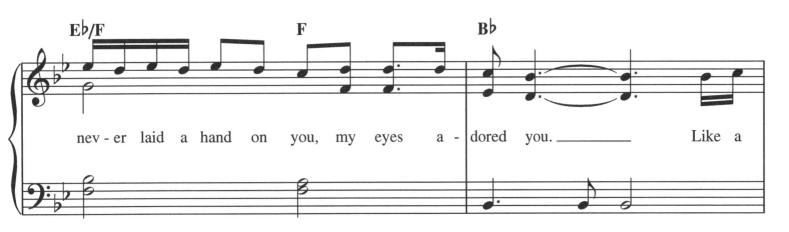

nev-er laid a hand on you, my eyes a-dored you. _____ Like a

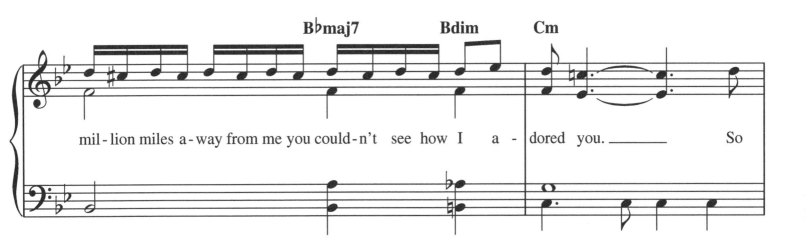

mil-lion miles a-way from me you could-n't see how I a-dored you. _____ So

close, so close and yet so far. _____ So

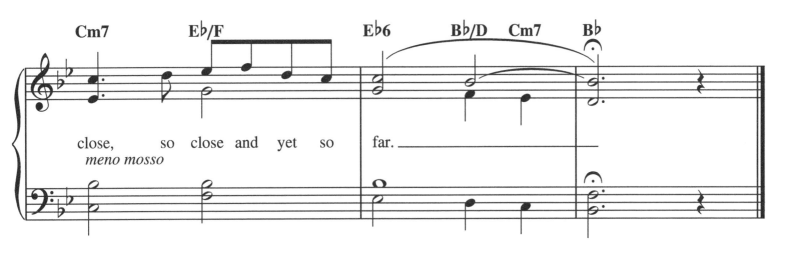

close, so close and yet so far. _____
meno mosso

RAG DOLL

Words and Music by ROBERT CREWE
and BOB GAUDIO

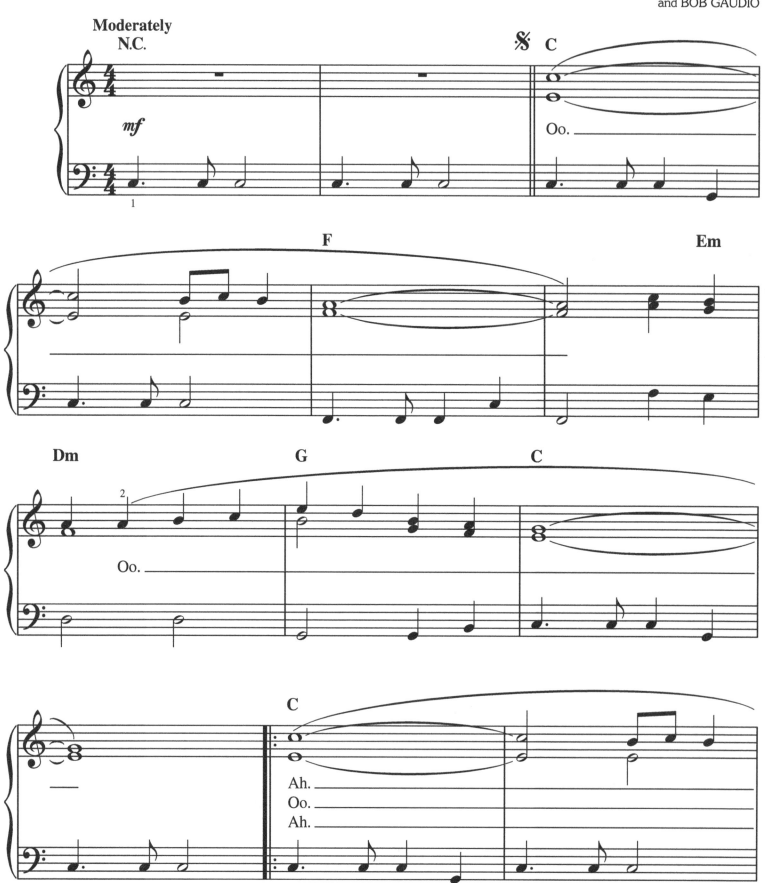

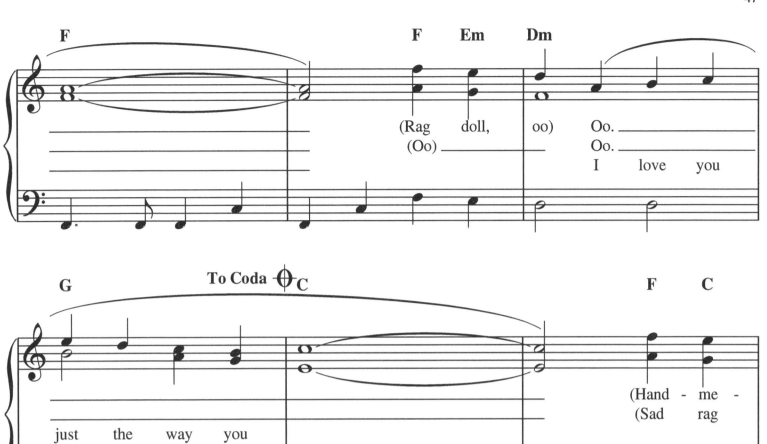

(Rag doll, oo) Oo. _____
(Oo) _____ Oo. _____
I love you

just the way you

(Hand - me -
(Sad rag

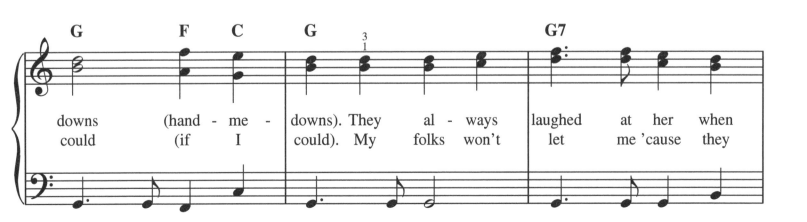

downs) When she was just a kid, her clothes were hand - me -
doll) I'd change her sad rags in - to glad rags if I

downs (hand - me - downs). They al - ways laughed at her when
could (if I could). My folks won't let me 'cause they

she came in - to town, called her
say that she's no good. She's a

rag
rag

doll, lit - tle
doll, such a

rag
rag

doll. Such a
doll. Though I

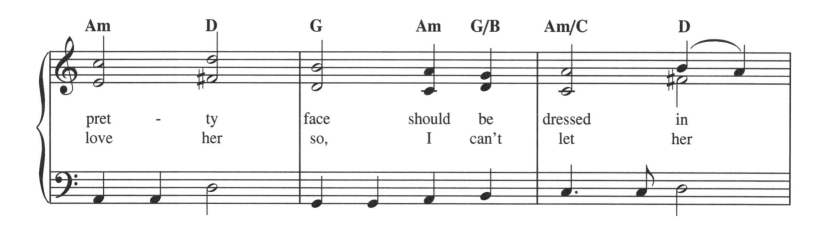

pret - ty
love her

face
so,

should be
I can't

dressed
let

in
her

1.
G

lace.

2.
G

D.S. al Coda

go.

CODA
C

are. _____

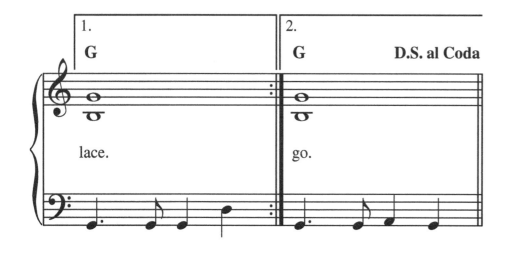

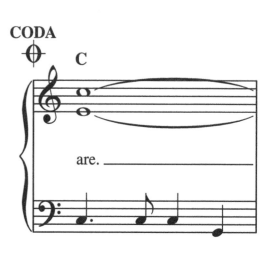

Oh.

(Rag   doll,   oo)   Oo.

Oh.

SHERRY

Words and Music by
BOB GAUDIO

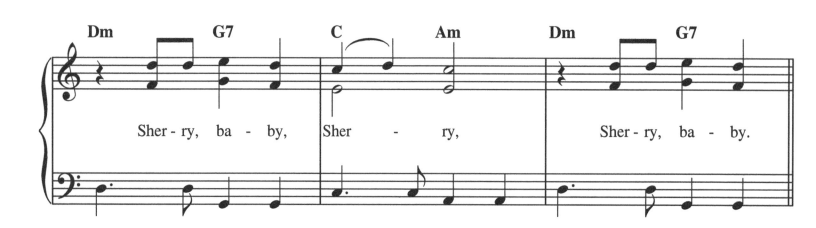

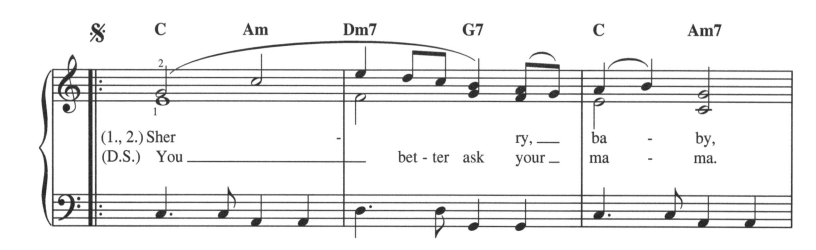

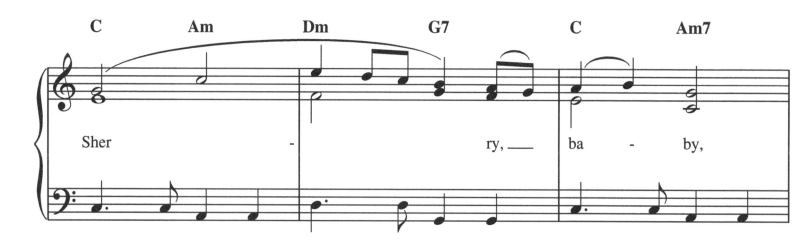

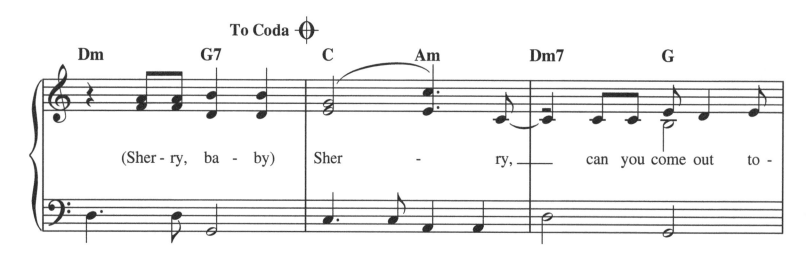

WHO LOVES YOU

Words and Music by ROBERT GAUDIO
and JUDY PARKER

Moderately fast Rock

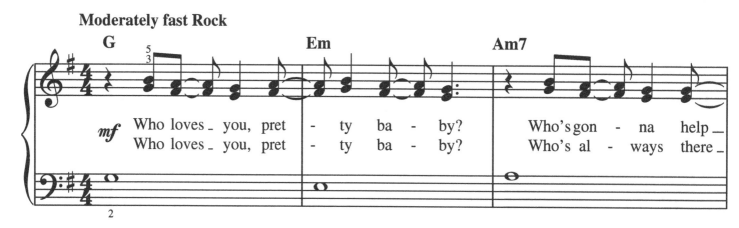

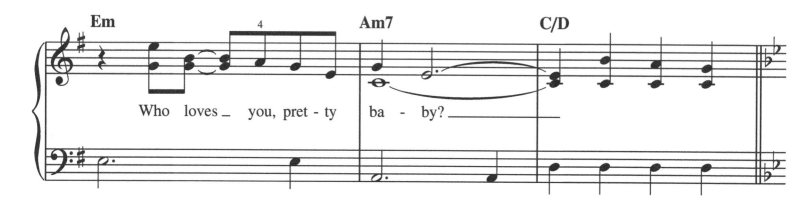

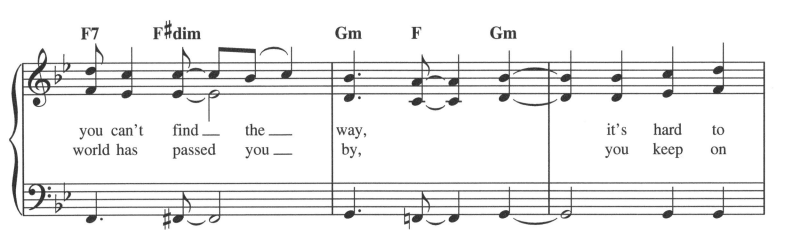

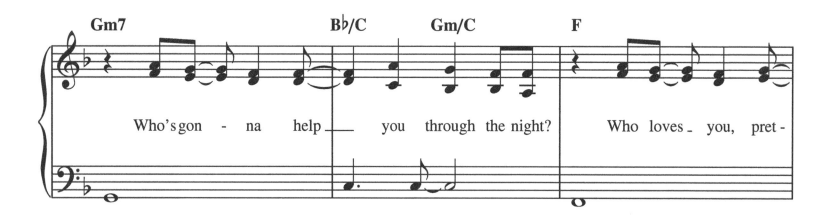

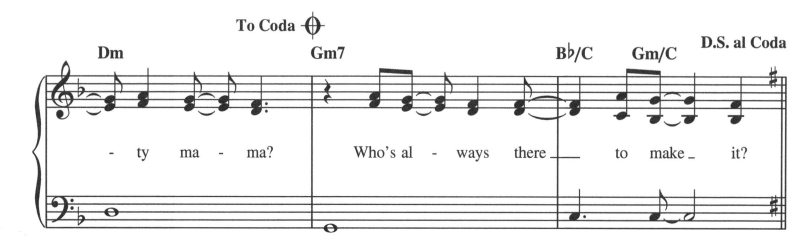

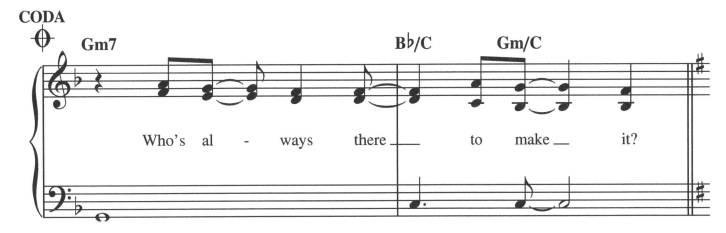

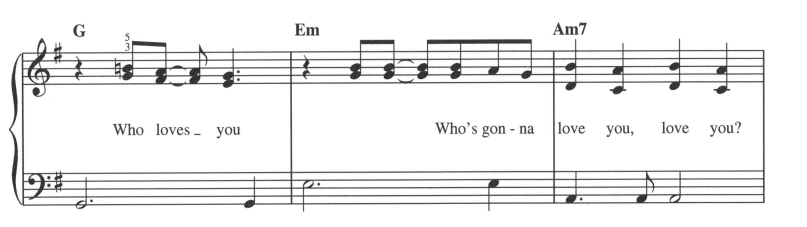

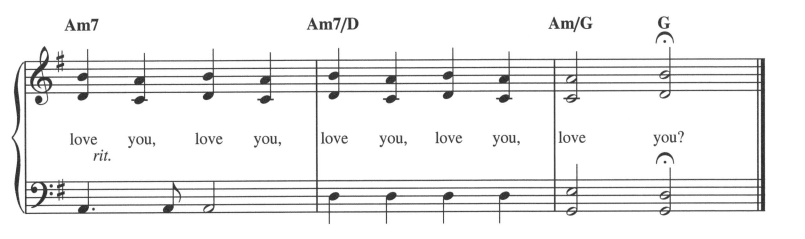

WORKING MY WAY BACK TO YOU

Words and Music by DENNY RANDELL
and SANDY LINZER

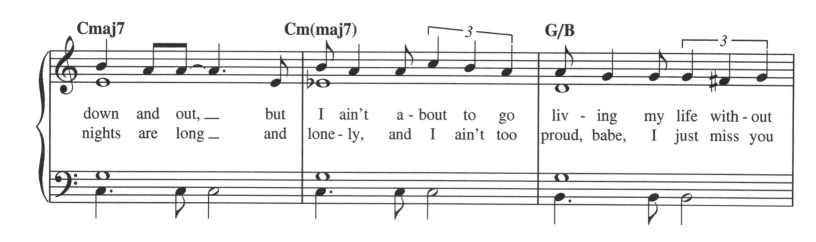

Cmaj7 ... **Cm(maj7)** ... **G/B**

down and out, ___ but I ain't a - bout to go liv - ing my life with - out
nights are long ___ and lone - ly, and I ain't too proud, babe, I just miss you

B♭dim ... **G** **C** ... **G** **C**

you. ___ Hey, for ev - 'ry day ___ I made you cry, ___ I'm
so. ___ Girl, but you're too proud, and you won't give in, ___ but

G **C** ... **1.** **B♭** **C6** **G**

pay - in', girl, ___ 'til the day that I die, ___ I'll keep
when I think ___ a - bout

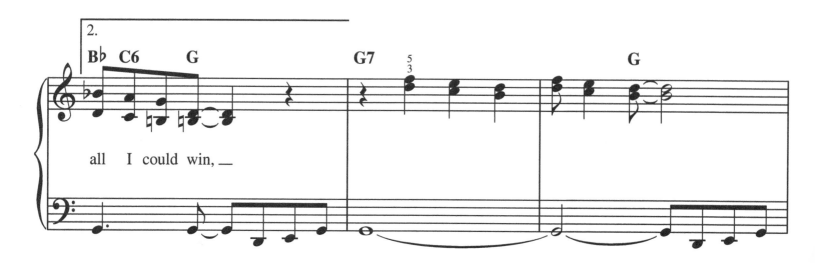

2. **B♭** **C6** **G** ... **G7** ... **G**

all I could win, ___

WALK LIKE A MAN

Words and Music by BOB CREWE
and BOB GAUDIO

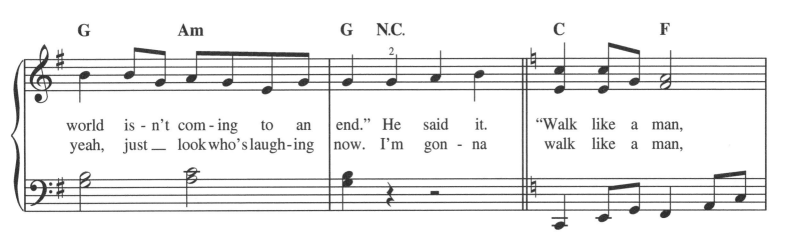

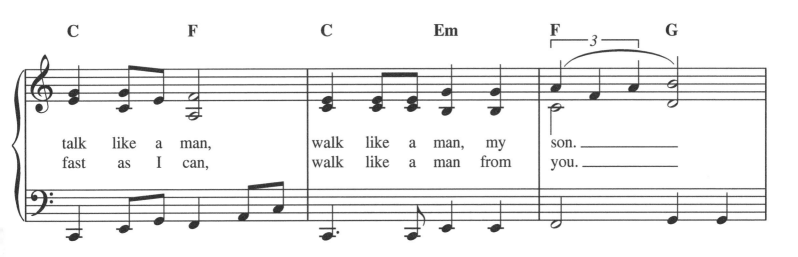